Everyman's Poetry

*Everyman, I will go with thee,
and be thy guide*

R. S. Thomas

Selected and edited by ANTHONY THWAITE

EVERYMAN

J. M. Dent · London

Introduction and other critical apparatus
© J.M. Dent 1996

Reprinted 1999, 2000

J.M.Dent
Orion Publishing Group
Orion House
5 Upper St Martin's Lane
London WC2H 9EA

Typeset by Deltatype Ltd, Ellesmere Port, Cheshire
Printed in Great Britain by
The Guernsey Press Co. Ltd, Guernsey, C.I.

British Library Cataloguing-in-Publication
Data is available upon request.

ISBN 0 460 87811 5

The author and publisher gratefully acknowledge the use of poems from *Later Poems*
(Macmillan London Ltd, 1983). *Experimenting With An Amen* (Macmillan London Ltd,
1986) and *Counterpoint* (Bloodaxe Books Ltd, 1990). Every effort has been made to trace all the
copyright holders, but if any have been inadvertently overlooked the publishers will be pleased to
make the necessary arrangement at the first opportunity.

Contents

Note on the Author and Editor

R. S. THOMAS was born in Cardiff in 1913 and brought up in Holyhead. He studied classics at the University of Wales, studied theology at St Michael's College, Llandaff, and then, ordained priest, served for the next forty years in six different rural parishes in Wales. He published his first book of poems in 1946 and since then has published over twenty books. He won the Heinemann Award in 1955, the Queen's Gold Medal for Poetry in 1964 and a Cholmondeley Award in 1978. He has also won three Welsh Arts Council Awards. Several of his books have been 'Choices' of the Poetry Book Society.

Apart from his own poetry, he has edited two anthologies, *The Batsford Book of Country Verse* (1961) and *The Penguin Book of Religious Verse* (1963), and selections of poems by George Herbert, Wordsworth, and Edward Thomas. He published an autobiography in Welsh, *Neb* ('no one' or 'anyone') in 1985.

He married the painter Mildred Eldridge in 1940, and they had one son. His wife died in 1991.

R. S. Thomas's *Collected Poems 1945–1990* was published in 1993, to mark the poet's eightieth birthday.

ANTHONY THWAITE was born in 1930 in England. He spent the years 1940–44 as a wartime evacuee in the USA. After graduating from Christ Church, Oxford, in 1955, he lectured in English literature at Tokyo University for two years. Since then he has been a BBC radio producer, literary editor in turn of the *Listener* and the *New Statesman* and co-editor of *Encounter* 1973–85. He has also taught in universities in Libya, Britain and the United States. He has published many books of poetry, most recently *The Dust of the World* (1994), and several books of criticism and anthologies. He is a Fellow of the Royal Society of Literature, and in 1990 was awarded the OBE for services to poetry.

Introduction

From the first, the poems of R. S. Thomas have been challenging statements about isolation, written in isolation. The early ones are clearly, uncompromisingly and in detail concerned with the people and landscapes of the remote depths of rural Wales in which, as a young clergyman in the Church in Wales (that is to say, the Welsh Anglican Church), R. S. Thomas chose to live and work after his ordination in 1937. Born in Cardiff, educated in Holyhead, he was not brought up in a Welsh-speaking background. But he firmly committed himself to learn the language while he was following his theological training at St Michael's College, Llandaff, so that he would be able to speak to his parishioners in their own first tongue.

Nevertheless, though he mastered Welsh for these purposes, he has always used English as the language of his poems. Further, he was an educated man moving among people he was not afraid to call 'peasants', however regretful he may have been to use that word. He was an Anglican minister living among parishioners who were mainly Nonconformists. He was troubled by religious doubts which could not easily be revealed to those whose faith was more fervent. And the places in which he lived and ministered were harsh, depopulated, deprived. All these factors underlined his sense of isolation.

His first two books, slender ones published by small Welsh firms, drew on work which in the early 1940s had appeared individually in journals which were not parochial or local: *Horizon, Life and Letters, Poetry London*; and in London anthologies – of *Modern Welsh Poetry* (Faber and Faber) and in *The Little Reviews Anthology* (Eyre and Spottiswoode). But it was not until the editor Alan Pryce-Jones and the novelist James Hanley separately recommended Thomas to Rupert Hart-Davis that there was a real breakthrough. *Song at the Year's Turning*, published by Hart-Davis in 1955, carried an introduction by John Betjeman – an English urban poet, not then at the peak of his fame and not, on the face of it, someone whom one would take to be an obvious admirer of such poems.

Betjeman said: 'This retiring poet had no wish for an introduction to be written to his poems, but his publisher believed that a "name" was needed to help sell the book. The "name" which has the honour to introduce this fine poet to a wider public will be forgotten long before that of R. S. Thomas.' From then on, Thomas became a force to be reckoned with in English poetry. The book was widely praised, often by unlikely people such as Kingsley Amis, who called Thomas 'one of the half-dozen best poets now writing in English'. He continued: 'To describe the effect of his work it is enough to say that he often moves to tears, and that certain lines of his impress themselves instantly, and perhaps ineradicably, upon the mind. His example reduces most modern verse to footling whimsy.' Buoyed up by such reactions, *Song at the Year's Turning* rapidly went into several impressions.

Since then, in the past forty years, Thomas's books have proliferated and his reputation has grown to such an extent that for some time he has been seriously presented as a candidate for the Nobel Prize for Literature. I doubt whether Thomas has been much moved, if at all, by this acclaim – whether emanating from Wales, which has honoured him in its own way, or from the world beyond. He is occasionally persuaded to go out and perform what he has wryly called 'cultural excesses on Saxon territory' (that is, read his poems to audiences in England). But, both before and after his retirement from the clergy in 1978, his isolation has largely prevailed.

Thomas's poems are an embodiment of Robert Frost's dictum: 'You can't be universal without being provincial.' From the 1940s until some time in the 1960s, this was almost literally true. The world of his invented type-character, Iago Prytherch – and of all those others, Twm, Cynddylan, Davies, Morgan, Ceridwen, Evans, Walter Llywarch, the Puws – is restricted, constricted, confined to a few narrow Welsh acres, struggling with a day-to-day life that has no horizons; only occasionally – and probably sentimentally – aware of some sort of historical inheritance which has been squandered, handed over long ago to the English.

Though he has in more recent years become a committed Welsh nationalist, Thomas is – in his poems – ambivalent and without illusions about the Welsh. Again and again he registers, sometimes bitterly, sometimes wearily, a conviction that his people have connived, been complicitous, in allowing their language to decline, their values to become money values, their country to become a quaint museum for tourists:

> Where can I go, then, from the smell
> Of decay, from the putrefying of a dead
> Nation? I have walked the shore
> For an hour and seen the English
> Scavenging among the remains
> Of our culture, covering the sand
> Like the tide and, with the roughness
> Of the tide, elbowing our language
> Into the grave that we have dug for it.

But there is affection too, and compassion, for the young, the old, the vulnerable, the hopeless. And, sometimes wincingly, there is a tart, bleak humour, as in the group of poems he published in 1974 called *What is a Welshman?*, which includes 'His Condescensions Are Short-Lived': a patronising recital about the shortcomings of the English, 'victims of their traditions', that the listener, the poet, gently but decisively punctures:

> I admired him
> there, as he sat nonchalantly
> in his chair, flicking the ash from
> his cigarette – supplied, by the way,
> as most things in Wales are
> supplied, by English wholesalers.

This quotation also serves to prompt some remarks about the stylistic change that gradually became apparent in Thomas's poems during the late 1960s and early 1970s: a gradual abandonment of metres which had until then been based, however loosely, on received forms. Some critics have been bothered by this, saying that the 'new' poems – however finely and intelligently written they may be – are simply lineated prose. On the page, this may seem to be so; but I would argue that, read aloud, they dictate their own distinct cadences.

More importantly, there came at the same time a change in the landscapes of the poems and in their preoccupations. To put it more brashly than Thomas ever does, he took on the big problem of God, not confined to narrow acres or even to Wales, but faced in a metaphysical landscape: faced as someone, or something, who was

probably universal, possibly non-existent, endlessly to be sought,
yearned for, questioned, argued with, perhaps settled for, never
quite rejected even at moments when he, or it, seemed to have
absconded:

> For some
> it is all darkness: for me, too,
> it is dark. But there are hands
> there I can take, voices to hear
> solider than the echoes
> without. And sometimes a strange light
> shines, purer than the moon,
> casting no shadow, that is
> the halo upon the bones
> of the pioneers who died for truth.

In what Thomas has called his 'linguistic confrontation with
ultimate reality', he has more and more come to a language and a
form both very plain and challengingly intense. He has never been
a poet to be quoted effectively in odd lines or blindingly memorable
phrases: he works his way through an observation, a situation or a
conundrum with a bleak wholeness. There is little of cheery
comfort in Thomas, early or late; but his is a voice that cannot be
ignored, however quietly he speaks. Right through his long career,
the mood and tone of his poems have been those of fastidious
brooding: he may seem to stand aloof; but as Ted Hughes, quoting
Lorca, has written, his poetry 'pierces the heart'.

ANTHONY THWAITE

R. S. Thomas

A Peasant

Iago Prytherch his name, though, be it allowed,
Just an ordinary man of the bald Welsh hills,
Who pens a few sheep in a gap of cloud.
Docking mangels, chipping the green skin
From the yellow bones with a half-witted grin
Of satisfaction, or churning the crude earth
To a stiff sea of clods that glint in the wind –
So are his days spent, his spittled mirth
Rarer than the sun that cracks the cheeks
Of the gaunt sky perhaps once in a week.
And then at night see him fixed in his chair
Motionless, except when he leans to gob in the fire.
There is something frightening in the vacancy of his mind.
His clothes, sour with years of sweat
And animal contact, shock the refined,
But affected, sense with their stark naturalness.
Yet this is your prototype, who, season by season
Against siege of rain and the wind's attrition,
Preserves his stock, an impregnable fortress
Not to be stormed even in death's confusion.
Remember him, then, for he, too, is a winner of wars,
Enduring like a tree under the curious stars.

Affinity

Consider this man in the field beneath,
Gaitered with mud, lost in his own breath,
Without joy, without sorrow,
Without children, without wife,
Stumbling insensitively from furrow to furrow,
A vague somnambulist; but hold your tears,
For his name also is written in the Book of Life.

Ransack your brainbox, pull out the drawers
That rot in your heart's dust, and what have you to give
To enrich his spirit or the way he lives?
From the standpoint of education or caste or creed
Is there anything to show that your essential need
Is less than his, who has the world for church,
And stands bare-headed in the woods' wide porch
Morning and evening to hear God's choir
Scatter their praises? Don't be taken in
By stinking garments or an aimless grin;
He also is human, and the same small star,
That lights you homeward, has inflamed his mind
With the old hunger, born of his kind.

Peasant Greeting

No speech; the raised hand affirms
All that is left unsaid
By the mute tongue and the unmoistened lips:
The land's patience and a tree's
Knotted endurance and
The heart's doubt whether to curse or bless,
All packed into a single gesture.
The knees crumble to the downward pull
Of the harsh earth, the eyes,
Fuddled with coldness, have no skill to smile.
Life's bitter jest is hollow, mirthless he slips
To his long grave under the wave of wind,
That breaks continually on the brittle ear.

A Priest to His People

Men of the hills, wantoners, men of Wales,
With your sheep and your pigs and your ponies, your sweaty
    females,
How I have hated you for your irreverence, your scorn even
Of the refinements of art and the mysteries of the Church,
I whose invective would spurt like a flame of fire
To be quenched always in the coldness of your stare.
Men of bone, wrenched from the bitter moorland,
Who have not yet shaken the moss from your savage skulls,
Or prayed the peat from your eyes,
Did you detect like an ewe or an ailing wether,
Driven into the undergrowth by the nagging flies,
My true heart wandering in a wood of lies?

You are curt and graceless, yet your sudden laughter
Is sharp and bright as a whipped pool,
When the wind strikes or the clouds are flying;
And all the devices of church and school
Have failed to cripple your unhallowed movements,
Or put a halter on your wild soul.
You are lean and spare, yet your strength is a mockery
Of the pale words in the black Book,
And why should you come like sparrows for prayer crumbs,
Whose hands can dabble in the world's blood?

I have taxed your ignorance of rhyme and sonnet,
Your want of deference to the painter's skill,
But I know, as I listen, that your speech has in it
The source of all poetry, clear as a rill
Bubbling from your lips; and what brushwork could equal
The artistry of your dwelling on the bare hill?

You will forgive, then, my initial hatred,
My first intolerance of your uncouth ways,
You who are indifferent to all that I can offer,
Caring not whether I blame or praise.

With your pigs and your sheep and your sons
    and holly-cheeked daughters
You will still continue to unwind your days
In a crude tapestry under the jealous heavens
To affront, bewilder, yet compel my gaze.

Iago Prytherch

Ah, Iago, my friend, whom the ignorant people thought
The last of your kind, since all the wealth you brought
From the age of gold was the yellow dust on your shoes,
Spilled by the meadow flowers, if you should choose
To wrest your barns from the wind and the weather's claws,
And break the hold of the moss on roof and gable;
If you can till your fields and stand to see
The world go by, a foolish tapestry
Scrawled by the times, and lead your mares to stable,
And dream your dream, and after the earth's laws
Order your life and faith, then you shall be
The first man of the new community.

Ire

Are you out, woman of the lean pelt,
And the table unlaid and bare
As a boar's backside, and the kettle
Loud as an old man, plagued with spittle,
Or a cat fight upon the stair?
The sink stinks, and the floor unscrubbed
Is no mirror for the preening sun
At the cracked lattice. Oh, the oven's cold
As Jesus' church, and never a bun
Lurks in the larder – Is this the way
You welcome your man from his long mowing
Of the harsh, unmannerly, mountain hay?

The Airy Tomb

Twm was a dunce at school, and was whipped and shaken
More than I care to say, but without avail,
For where one man can lead a horse to the pail
Twenty can't make him drink what is not to his mind,
And books and sums were poison to Tomos, he was stone blind
To the print's magic; yet his grass-green eye
Missed nor swoop nor swerve of the hawk's wing
Past the high window, and the breeze could bring.
Above the babble of the room's uproar,
Songs to his ear from the sun-dusted moor,
The grey curlew's whistle and the shrill, far cry
Of circling buzzard . . . This was Twm at school,
Subject to nothing but the sky and the wind's rule.
And then at fourteen term ended and the lad was free.
Scatheless as when he entered, he could write and spell
No more than the clouds could or the dribbling rain,
That scrawled vague messages on the window pane.

And so he returned to the Bwlch to help his father
With the rough work of the farm, to ditch, and gather
The slick ewes from the hill; to milk the cow,
And coax the mare that dragged the discordant plough.
Stepping with one stride thus from boy to man,
His school books finished with, he now began
Learning what none could teach but the hill people
In that cold country, where grass and tree
Are a green heritage more rich and rare
Than a queen's emerald or an untouched maid.
It were as well to bring the tup to the wild mare,
Or put the heron and the hen to couple,
As mate a stranger from the fat plain
With that gaunt wilderness, where snow is laid
Deadly as leprosy till the first of May,
And a man counts himself lucky if All Saints' Day
Finds his oats hived in the tottering barn.
But Tomos took to the life like a hillman born;

His work was play after the dull school, and hands,
Shamed by the pen's awkwardness, toyed with the fleece
Of ewe and wether; eyes found a new peace
Tracing the poems, which the rooks wrote in the sky.

So his shadow lengthened, and the years sped by
With the wind's quickness; Twm had turned nineteen,
When his father sickened and at the week's end died,
Leaving him heir to the lean patch of land,
Pinned to the hill-top, and the cloudy acres,
Kept as a sheep-walk. At his mother's side
He stood in the graveyard, where the undertaker
Sprinkled earth rubble with a loud tattoo
On the cheap coffin; but his heart was hurt
By the gash in the ground, and too few, too few
Were the tears that he dropped for that lonely man
Beginning his journey to annihilation.
He had seen sheep rotting in the wind and sun,
And a hawk floating in a bubbling pool,
Its weedy entrails mocking the breast
Laced with bright water; but the dead and living
Moved hand in hand on the mountain crest
In the calm circle of taking and giving.
A wide sepulchre of brisk, blue air
Was the beasts' portion, but a mortal's lot
The boards' strictness, and an ugly scar
On the earth's surface, till the deliberate sod
Sealed off for ever the green land he trod.

But the swift grass, that covered the unsightly wound
In the prim churchyard, healed Tomos' mind
Of its grave-sickness, and December shadows
Dwindled to nothingness in the spring meadows,
That were blowsy with orchis and the loose bog-cotton.
Then the sun strengthened and the hush of June
Settled like lichen on the thick-timbered house,
Where Twm and his mother ate face to face
At the bare table, and each tick of the clock
Was a nail knocked in the lid of the coffin
Of that pale, spent woman, who sat with death

Jogging her elbow through the hot, still days
Of July and August, or passed like a ghost
By the scurrying poultry – it was ever her boast
Not to stay one winter with the goodman cold
In his callous bed. Twm was bumpkin blind
To the vain hysteria of a woman's mind,
And prated of sheep fairs, but the first frost came
To prove how ungarnished was the truth she told.

Can you picture Tomos now in the house alone,
The room silent, and the last mourner gone
Down the hill pathway? Did he sit by the flame
Of his turf fire and watch till dawn
The slow crumbling of the world he had known?
Did he rebuild out of the ragged embers
A new life, tempered to the sting of sorrow?
Twm went to bed and woke on the grey morrow
To the usual jobbery in sty and stable;
Cleaned out the cow-house, harnessed the mare,
And went prospecting with the keen ploughshare.
Yet sometimes the day was dark, and the clouds remembered,
Herded in the bare lanes of sky, the funeral rite,
And Tomos about the house or set at table
Was aware of something for which he had no name,
Though the one tree, which dripped through the winter night
With a clock's constancy, tried hard to tell
The insensitive mind what the heart knew well.

But March squalls, making the windows rattle,
Blew great gaps in his thoughts, till April followed
With a new sweetness, that set the streams gossiping.
On Easter Day he heard the first warbler sing
In the quick ash by the door, and the snow made room
On the sharp turf for the first fumbling lamb.
Docking and grading now until after dark
In the green field or fold, there was too much work
For the mind to wander, though the robin wove
In the young hazel a sweet tale of love.
And what is love to an uncultured youth
In the desolate pastures, but the itch of cattle

At set times and seasons? Twm rarely went down
With his gay neighbours to the petticoat town
In a crook of the valley, and his mind was free
Of the dream pictures which lead to romance.
Hearts and arrows, scribbled at the lane's entrance,
Were a meaningless symbol, as esoteric
As his school fractions; the one language he knew
Was the shrill scream in the dark, the shadow within the
    shadow,
The glimmer of flesh, deadly as mistletoe.

Of course there was talk in the parish, girls stood at their doors
In November evenings, their glances busy as moths
Round that far window; and some, whom passion made bolder
As the buds opened, lagged in the bottom meadow
And coughed and called. But never a voice replied
From that grim house, nailed to the mountain side,
For Tomos was up with the lambs, or stealthily hoarding
The last light from the sky in his soul's crannies.
So the tongues still wagged, and Tomos became a story
To please a neighbour with, or raise the laughter
In the lewd tavern, for folk cannot abide
The inscrutable riddle, posed by their own kin.
And you, hypocrite reader, at ease in your chair,
Do not mock their conduct, for are you not also weary
Of this odd tale, preferring the usual climax?
He was not well-favoured, you think, nor gay, nor rich,
But surely it happened that one of those supple bitches
With the sly haunches angled him into her net
At the male season, or, what is perhaps more romantic,
Some lily-white maid, a clerk or a minister's daughter,
With delicate hands, and eyes brittle as flowers
Or curved sea-shells, taught him the tender airs
Of a true gallant?
            No, no, you must face the fact
Of his long life alone in that crumbling house
With winds rending the joints, and the grey rain's claws
Sharp in the thatch; of his work up on the moors
With the moon for candle, and the shrill rabble of stars
Crowding his shoulders. For Twm was true to his fate,

That wound solitary as a brook through the crimson heather,
Trodden only by sheep, where youth and age
Met in the circle of a buzzard's flight
Round the blue axle of heaven; and a fortnight gone
Was the shy soul from the festering flesh and bone
When they found him there, entombed in the lucid weather.

Spring Equinox

Do not say, referring to the sun,
'Its journey northward has begun,'
As though it were a bird, annually migrating,
That now returns to build in the rich trees
Its nest of golden grass. Do not belie
Its lusty health with words such as imply
A pallid invalid recuperating.
The age demands the facts, therefore be brief –
Others will sense the simile – and say:
'We are turning towards the sun's indifferent ray.'

The Welsh Hill Country

Too far for you to see
The fluke and the foot-rot and the fat maggot
Gnawing the skin from the small bones,
The sheep are grazing at Bwlch-y-Fedwen,
Arranged romantically in the usual manner
On a bleak background of bald stone.

Too far for you to see
The moss and the mould on the cold chimneys,
The nettles growing through the cracked doors,
The houses stand empty at Nant-yr-Eira,
There are holes in the roofs that are thatched with sunlight,
And the fields are reverting to the bare moor.

Too far, too far to see
The set of his eyes and the slow phthisis
Wasting his frame under the ripped coat,
There's a man still farming at Ty'n-y-Fawnog,
Contributing grimly to the accepted pattern,
The embryo music dead in his throat.

Song for Gwydion

When I was a child and the soft flesh was forming
Quietly as snow on the bare boughs of bone,
My father brought me trout from the green river
From whose chill lips the water song had flown.

Dull grew their eyes, the beautiful, blithe garland
Of stipples faded, as light shocked the brain;
They were the first sweet sacrifice I tasted,
A young god, ignorant of the blood's stain.

The Old Language

England, what have you done to make the speech
My fathers used a stranger at my lips,
An offence to the ear, a shackle on the tongue
That would fit new thoughts to an abiding tune?
Answer me now. The workshop where they wrought
Stands idle, and thick dust covers their tools.
The blue metal of streams, the copper and gold
Seams in the wood are all unquarried; the leaves'
Intricate filigree falls, and who shall renew
Its brisk pattern? When spring wakens the hearts
Of the young children to sing, what song shall be theirs?

The Evacuee

She woke up under a loose quilt
Of leaf patterns, woven by the light
At the small window, busy with the boughs
Of a young cherry; but wearily she lay,
Waiting for the syren, slow to trust
Nature's deceptive peace, and then afraid
Of the long silence, she would have crept
Uneasily from the bedroom with its frieze
Of fresh sunlight, had not a cock crowed,
Shattering the surface of that limpid pool
Of stillness, and before the ripples died
One by one in the field's shallows,
The farm awoke with uninhibited din.

And now the noise and not the silence drew her
Down the bare stairs at great speed.
The sounds and voices were a rough sheet
Waiting to catch her, as though she leaped
From a scorched story of the charred past.

And there the table and the gallery
Of farm faces trying to be kind
Beckoned her nearer, and she sat down
Under an awning of salt hams.

And so she grew, a shy bird in the nest
Of welcome that was built about her,
Home now after so long away
In the flowerless streets of the drab town.
The men watched her busy with the hens,
The soft flesh ripening warm as corn
On the sticks of limbs, the grey eyes clear,
Rinsed with dew of their long dread.
The men watched her, and, nodding, smiled
With earth's charity, patient and strong.

Depopulation of the Hills

Leave it, leave it – the hole under the door
Was a mouth through which the rough wind spoke
Ever more sharply; the dank hand
Of age was busy on the walls
Scrawling in blurred characters
Messages of hate and fear.

Leave it, leave it – the cold rain began
At summer end – there is no road
Over the bog, and winter comes
With mud above the axletree.

Leave it, leave it – the rain dripped
Day and night from the patched roof
Sagging beneath its load of sky.

Did the earth help them, time befriend
These last survivors? Did the spring grass
Heal winter's ravages? The grass
Wrecked them in its draughty tides,
Grew from the chimney-stack like smoke,
Burned its way through the weak timbers.
That was nature's jest, the sides
Of the old hulk cracked, but not with mirth.

The Gap in the Hedge

That man, Prytherch, with the torn cap,
I saw him often, framed in the gap
Between two hazels with his sharp eyes,
Bright as thorns, watching the sunrise
Filling the valley with its pale yellow
Light, where the sheep and the lambs went haloed
With grey mist lifting from the dew.
Or was it a likeness that the twigs drew
With bold pencilling upon that bare
Piece of sky? For he's still there
At early morning, when the light is right
And I look up suddenly at a bird's flight.

Cynddylan on a Tractor

Ah, you should see Cynddylan on a tractor.
Gone the old look that yoked him to the soil;
He's a new man now, part of the machine,
His nerves of metal and his blood oil.
The clutch curses, but the gears obey
His least bidding, and lo, he's away
Out of the farmyard, scattering hens.
Riding to work now as a great man should,
He is the knight at arms breaking the fields'
Mirror of silence, emptying the wood
Of foxes and squirrels and bright jays.
The sun comes over the tall trees
Kindling all the hedges, but not for him
Who runs his engine on a different fuel.
And all the birds are singing, bills wide in vain,
As Cynddylan passes proudly up the lane.

The Hill Farmer Speaks

I am the farmer, stripped of love
And thought and grace by the land's hardness;
But what I am saying over the fields'
Desolate acres, rough with dew,
Is, Listen, listen, I am a man like you.

The wind goes over the hill pastures
Year after year, and the ewes starve,
Milkless, for want of the new grass.
And I starve, too, for something the spring
Can never foster in veins run dry.

The pig is a friend, the cattle's breath
Mingles with mine in the still lanes;
I wear it willingly like a cloak
To shelter me from your curious gaze.

The hens go in and out at the door
From sun to shadow, as stray thoughts pass
Over the floor of my wide skull.
The dirt is under my cracked nails;
The tale of my life is smirched with dung;
The phlegm rattles. But what I am saying
Over the grasses rough with dew
Is, Listen, listen, I am a man like you.

Death of a Peasant

You remember Davies? He died, you know,
With his face to the wall, as the manner is
Of the poor peasant in his stone croft
On the Welsh hills. I recall the room
Under the slates, and the smirched snow
Of the wide bed in which he lay,
Lonely as an ewe that is sick to lamb
In the hard weather of mid-March.
I remember also the trapped wind
Tearing the curtains, and the wild light's
Frequent hysteria upon the floor,
The bare floor without a rug
Or mat to soften the loud tread
Of neighbours crossing the uneasy boards
To peer at Davies with gruff words
Of meaningless comfort, before they turned
Heartless away from the stale smell
Of death in league with those dank walls.

The Unborn Daughter

On her unborn in the vast circle
Concentric with our finite lives;
On her unborn, her name uncurling
Like a young fern within the mind;
On her unclothed with flesh or beauty
In the womb's darkness, I bestow
The formal influence of the will,
The wayward influence of the heart,
Weaving upon her fluid bones
The subtle fabric of her being,
Hair, hands and eyes, the body's texture,
Shot with the glory of the soul.

Welsh Landscape

To live in Wales is to be conscious
At dusk of the spilled blood
That went to the making of the wild sky,
Dyeing the immaculate rivers
In all their courses.
It is to be aware,
Above the noisy tractor
And hum of the machine
Of strife in the strung woods,
Vibrant with sped arrows.
You cannot live in the present,
At least not in Wales.
There is the language for instance,
The soft consonants
Strange to the ear.
There are cries in the dark at night
As owls answer the moon,
And thick ambush of shadows,
Hushed at the fields' corners.
There is no present in Wales,
And no future;
There is only the past,
Brittle with relics,
Wind-bitten towers and castles
With sham ghosts;
Mouldering quarries and mines;
And an impotent people,
Sick with inbreeding,
Worrying the carcase of an old song.

Valediction

You failed me, farmer, I was afraid you would
The day I saw you loitering with the cows,
Yourself one of them but for the smile,
Vague as moonlight, cast upon your face
From some dim source, whose nature I mistook.
The hills had grace, the light clothed them
With wild beauty, so that I thought,
Watching the pattern of your slow wake
Through seas of dew, that you yourself
Wore that same beauty by the right of birth.

I know now, many a time since
Hurt by your spite or guile that is more sharp
Than stinging hail and treacherous
As white frost forming after a day
Of smiling warmth, that your uncouthness has
No kinship with the earth, where all is forgiven,
All is requited in the seasonal round
Of sun and rain, healing the year's scars.

Unnatural and inhuman, your wild ways
Are not sanctioned; you are condemned
By man's potential stature. The two things
That could redeem your ignorance, the beauty
And grace that trees and flowers labour to teach,
Were never yours, you shut your heart against them.
You stopped your ears to the soft influence
Of birds, preferring the dull tone
Of the thick blood, the loud, unlovely rattle
Of mucus in the throat, the shallow stream
Of neighbours' trivial talk.
                 For this I leave you
Alone in your harsh acres, herding pennies
Into a sock to serve you for a pillow
Through the long night that waits upon your span.

The Labourer

There he goes, tacking against the fields'
Uneasy tides. What have the centuries done
To change him? The same garments, frayed with light
Or seamed with rain, cling to the wind-scoured bones
And shame him in the eyes of the spruce birds.
Once it was ignorance, then need, but now
Habit that drapes him on a bush of cloud
For life to mock at, while the noisy surf
Of people dins far off at the world's rim.
He has been here since life began, a vague
Movement among the roots of the young grass.
Bend down and peer beneath the twigs of hair,
And look into the hard eyes, flecked with care;
What do you see? Notice the twitching hands,
Veined like a leaf, and tough bark of the limbs,
Wrinkled and gnarled, and tell me what you think.
A wild tree still, whose seasons are not yours,
The slow heart beating to the hidden pulse
Of the strong sap, the feet firm in the soil?
No, no, a man like you, but blind with tears
Of sweat to the bright star that draws you on.

The One Furrow

When I was young, I went to school
With pencil and foot-rule
Sponge and slate,
And sat on a tall stool
At learning's gate.

When I was older, the gate swung wide;
Clever and keen-eyed
In I pressed,
But found in the mind's pride
No peace, no rest.

Then who was it taught me back to go
To cattle and barrow,
Field and plough;
To keep to the one furrow,
As I do now?

An Old Woman

Her days are measured out in pails of water,
Drawn from the pump, while drops of milkless tea,
Brewed in the cup, record the passing hours.
Yet neither tea nor heat of the small fire,
Its few red petals drooping in the grate,
Can stop the ice that forms within her veins,
And knots the blood and clouds the clear, blue eye.
At edge of night she sits in the one chair,
That mocks the frailness of her bones, and stares
Out of the leaded window at the moon,
That amber serpent swallowing an egg;
Footsteps she hears not, and no longer sees
The crop of faces blooming in the hedge
When curious children cluster in the dusk,
Vision being weak and ear-drums stiff with age.
And yet if neighbours call she leans and snatches
The crumbs of gossip from their busy lips,
Sharp as a bird, and now and then she laughs,
A high, shrill, mirthless laugh, half cough, half whistle,
Tuneless and dry as east wind through a thistle.

Song at the Year's Turning

Shelley dreamed it. Now the dream decays.
The props crumble. The familiar ways
Are stale with tears trodden underfoot.
The heart's flower withers at the root.
Bury it, then, in history's sterile dust.
The slow years shall tame your tawny lust.

Love deceived him; what is there to say
The mind brought you by a better way
To this despair? Lost in the world's wood
You cannot stanch the bright menstrual blood.
The earth sickens; under naked boughs
The frost comes to barb your broken vows.

Is there blessing? Light's peculiar grace
In cold splendour robes this tortured place
For strange marriage. Voices in the wind
Weave a garland where a mortal sinned.
Winter rots you; who is there to blame?
The new grass shall purge you in its flame.

A Person from Porlock

There came a knocking at the front door,
The eternal, nameless caller at the door;
The sound pierced the still hall,
But not the stillness about his brain.
It came again. He arose, pacing the floor
Strewn with books, his mind big with the poem
Soon to be born, his nerves tense to endure
The long torture of delayed birth.

Delayed birth: the embryo maimed in the womb
By the casual caller, the chance cipher that jogs
The poet's elbow, spilling the cupped dream.

The encounter over, he came, seeking his room;
Seeking the contact with his lost self;
Groping his way endlessly back
On the poem's path, calling by name
The foetus stifling in the mind's gloom.

January

The fox drags its wounded belly
Over the snow, the crimson seeds
Of blood burst with a mild explosion,
Soft as excrement, bold as roses.

Over the snow that feels no pity,
Whose white hands can give no healing,
The fox drags its wounded belly.

Priest and Peasant

You are ill, Davies, ill in mind;
An old canker, to your kind
Peculiar, has laid waste the brain's
Potential richness in delight
And beauty; and your body grows
Awry like an old thorn for lack
Of the soil's depth; and sickness there
Uncurls slowly its small tongues
Of fungus that shall, thickening, swell
And choke you, while your few leaves
Are green still.
                                    And so you work
In the wet fields and suffer pain
And loneliness as a tree takes
The night's darkness, the day's rain;
While I watch you, and pray for you,
And so increase my small store
Of credit in the bank of God,
Who sees you suffer and me pray
And touches you with the sun's ray,
That heals not, yet blinds my eyes
And seals my lips as Job's were sealed
Imperiously in the old days.

The Last of the Peasantry

What does he know? moving through the fields
And the wood's echoing cloisters
With a beast's gait, hunger in his eyes
Only for what the flat earth supplies;
His wisdom dwindled to a small gift
For handling stock, planting a few seeds
To ripen slowly in the warm breath
Of an old God to whom he never prays.

Moving through the fields, or still at home,
Dwarfed by his shadow on the bright wall,
His face is lit always from without,
The sun by day, the red fire at night;
Within is dark and bare, the grey ash
Is cold now, blow on it as you will.

Border Blues

All along the border the winds blow
Eastward from Wales, and the rivers flow
Eastward from Wales with the roads and the railways,
Reversing the path of the old migrations.
And the winds say, It is April, bringing scents
Of dead heroes and dead saints.
But the rivers are surly with brown water
Running amok, and the men to tame them
Are walking the streets of a far town.

Spring is here and the birds are singing;
Spring is here and the bells are ringing
In country churches, but not for a bride.
The sexton breaks the unleavened earth
Over the grave.
                          Are there none to marry?
There is still an Olwen teasing a smile
Of bright flowers out of the grass,
Olwen in nylons. Quick, quick,
Marry her someone. But Arthur leers
And turns again to the cramped kitchen
Where the old mother sits with her sons and daughters
At the round table. Ysbaddaden Penkawr's
Cunning was childish measured with hers.

*

I was going up the road and Beuno beside me
Talking in Latin and old Welsh,
When a volley of voices struck us; I turned,
But Beuno had vanished, and in his place
There stood the ladies from the council houses:
Blue eyes and Birmingham yellow
Hair, and the ritual murder of vowels.
Excuse me, I said, I have an appointment

On the high moors; it's the first of May
And I must go the way of my fathers
Despite the loneli – you might say rudeness.

Sheep song round me in the strong light;
The ancient traffic of glad birds
Returning to breed in the green sphagnum –
What am I doing up here alone
But paying homage to a bleak, stone
Monument to an evicted people?
Go back, go back; from the rough heather
The grouse repels me, and with slow step
I turn to go, but down not back.

*

Eryr Pengwern, penngarn llwyt heno . . .
We still come in by the Welsh gate, but it's a long way
To Shrewsbury now from the Welsh border.
There's the train, of course, but I like the 'buses;
We go each Christmas to the pantomime:
It was 'The Babes' this year, all about nature.
On the way back, when we reached the hills –
All black they were with a trimming of stars –
Some of the old ones got sentimental,
Singing Pantycelyn; but we soon drowned them;
It's funny, these new tunes are easy to learn.
We reached home at last, but *diawl!* I was tired.
And to think that my grand-dad walked it each year,
Scythe on shoulder to mow the hay,
And his own waiting when he got back.

*

Mi sydd fachgen ifanc, ffôl,
Yn byw yn ôl fy ffansi.
Riding on a tractor,
Whistling tunes
From the world's dance-halls;

Dreaming of the girl, Ceridwen,
With the red lips,
And red nails.
Coming in late,
Rising early
To flog the carcase
Of the brute earth;
A lad of the 'fifties,
Gay, tough,
I sit, as my fathers have done,
In the back pews on Sundays
And have fun.

*

Going by the long way round the hedges;
Speaking to no one, looking north
At every corner, she comes from the wise man.
Five lengths of yarn from palm to elbow
Wound round the throat, then measured again
Till the yarn shrinks, a cure for jaundice.

Hush, not a word. When we've finished milking
And the stars are quiet, we'll get out the car
And go to Llangurig; the mare's bewitched
Down in the pasture, letting feg
Tarnish the mirror of bright grass.

*

Six drops in a bottle,
And an old rhyme
Scatched on a slate
With stone pencil:
Abracadabra,
Count three, count nine;
Bury it in your neighbour's field
At bed-time.

*

As I was saying, I don't hold with war
Myself, but when you join your unit
Send me some of your brass buttons
And I'll have a shot at the old hare
In the top meadow, for the black cow
Is a pint short each morning now.

Be careful, mind where you're going.
These headlights dazzle, their bright blade
Reaps us a rich harvest of shadow.
But when they have gone, it is darker still,
And the vixen moves under the hill
With a new boldness, fretting her lust
To rawness on the unchristened grass.
It's easy to stray from the main road
And find yourself at the old *domen*.
I once heard footsteps in the leaves,
And saw men hiding behind the trunks
Of the trees. I never went there again,
Though that was at night, and the night is different.
The day divides us, but at night
We meet in the inn and warm our hearts
At the red beer with yarn and song;
Despite our speech we are not English,
And our wit is sharp as an axe yet,
Finding the bone beneath the skin
And the soft marrow in the bone.
We are not English . . . *Ni bydd diwedd*
Byth ar swn y delyn aur.
Though the strings are broken, and time sets
The barbed wire in their place,
The tune endures; on the cracked screen
Of life our shadows are large still
In history's fierce afterglow.

Evans

Evans? Yes, many a time
I came down his bare flight
Of stairs into the gaunt kitchen
With its wood fire, where crickets sang
Accompaniment to the black kettle's
Whine, and so into the cold
Dark to smother in the thick tide
Of night that drifted about the walls
Of his stark farm on the hill ridge.

It was not the dark filling my eyes
And mouth appalled me; not even the drip
Of rain like blood from the one tree
Weather-tortured. It was the dark
Silting the veins of that sick man
I left stranded upon the vast
And lonely shore of his bleak bed.

The Country Clergy

I see them working in old rectories
By the sun's light, by candlelight,
Venerable men, their black cloth
A little dusty, a little green
With holy mildew. And yet their skulls,
Ripening over so many prayers,
Toppled into the same grave
With oafs and yokels. They left no books,
Memorial to their lonely thought
In grey parishes; rather they wrote
On men's hearts and in the minds
Of young children sublime words
Too soon forgotten. God in his time
Or out of time will correct this.

Ap Huw's Testament

There are four verses to put down
For the four people in my life,
Father, mother, wife

And the one child. Let me begin
With her of the immaculate brow
My wife; she loves me. I know how.

My mother gave me the breast's milk
Generously, but grew mean after,
Envying me my detached laughter.

My father was a passionate man,
Wrecked after leaving the sea
In her love's shallows. He grieves in me.

What shall I say of my boy,
Tall, fair? He is young yet;
Keep his feet free of the world's net.

Iago Prytherch

Iago Prytherch, forgive my naming you.
You are so far in your small fields
From the world's eye, sharpening your blade
On a cloud's edge, no one will tell you
How I made fun of you, or pitied either
Your long soliloquies, crouched at your slow
And patient surgery under the faint
November rays of the sun's lamp.

Made fun of you? That was their graceless
Accusation, because I took
Your rags for theme, because I showed them
Your thought's bareness; science and art,
The mind's furniture, having no chance
To install themselves, because of the great
Draught of nature sweeping the skull.

Fun? Pity? No word can describe
My true feelings. I passed and saw you
Labouring there, your dark figure
Marring the simple geometry
Of the square fields with its gaunt question.
My poems were made in its long shadow
Falling coldly across the page.

Meet the Family

John One takes his place at the table,
He is the first part of the fable;
His eyes are dry as a dead leaf.
Look on him and learn grief.

John Two stands in the door
Dumb; you have seen that face before
Leaning out of the dark past,
Tortured in thought's bitter blast.

John Three is still outside
Drooling where the daylight died
On the wet stones; his hands are crossed
In mourning for a playmate lost.

John All and his lean wife,
Whose forced complicity gave life
To each loathed foetus, stare from the wall,
Dead not absent. The night falls.

Walter Llywarch

I am, as you know, Walter Llywarch,
Born in Wales of approved parents,
Well goitred, round in the bum,
Sure prey of the slow virus
Bred in quarries of grey rain.

Born in autumn at the right time
For hearing stories from the cracked lips
Of old folk dreaming of summer,
I piled them on to the bare hearth
Of my own fancy to make a blaze
To warm myself, but achieved only
The smoke's acid that brings the smart
Of false tears into the eyes.

Months of fog, months of drizzle;
Thought wrapped in the grey cocoon
Of race, of place, awaiting the sun's
Coming, but when the sun came,
Touching the hills with a hot hand,
Wings were spread only to fly
Round and round in a cramped cage
Or beat in vain at the sky's window.

School in the week, on Sunday chapel:
Tales of a land fairer than this
Were not so tall, for others had proved it
Without the grave's passport, they sent
The fruit home for ourselves to taste.

Walter Llywarch – the words were a name
On a lost letter that never came
For one who waited in the long queue
Of life that wound through a Welsh valley.
I took instead, as others had done
Before, a wife from the back pews

In chapel, rather to share the rain
Of winter evenings, than to intrude
On her pale body; and yet we lay
For warmth together and laughed to hear
Each new child's cry of despair.

Genealogy

I was the dweller in the long cave
Of darkness, lining it with the forms
Of bulls. My hand matured early,

But turned to violence: I was the man
Watching later at the grim ford,
Armed with resentment; the quick stream

Remembers at sunset the raw crime.
The deed pursued me; I was the king
At the church keyhole, who saw death

Loping towards me. From that hour
I fought for right, with the proud chiefs
Setting my name to the broad treaties.

I marched to Bosworth with the Welsh lords
To victory, but regretted after
The white house at the wood's heart.

I was the stranger in the new town,
Whose purse of tears was soon spent;
I filled it with a solider coin

At the dark sources. I stand now
In the hard light of the brief day
Without roots, but with many branches.

Ninetieth Birthday

You go up the long track
That will take a car, but is best walked
On slow foot, noting the lichen
That writes history on the page
Of the grey rock. Trees are about you
At first, but yield to the green bracken,
The nightjar's house: you can hear it spin
On warm evenings; it is still now
In the noonday heat, only the lesser
Voices sound, blue-fly and gnat
And the stream's whisper. As the road climbs,
You will pause for breath and the far sea's
Signal will flash, till you turn again
To the steep track, buttressed with cloud.

And there at the top that old woman,
Born almost a century back
In that stone farm, awaits your coming;
Waits for the news of the lost village
She thinks she knows, a place that exists
In her memory only.
                              You bring her greeting
And praise for having lasted so long
With time's knife shaving the bone.
Yet no bridge joins her own
World with yours, all you can do
Is lean kindly across the abyss
To hear words that were once wise.

Too Late

I would have spared you this, Prytherch;
You were like a child to me.
I would have seen you poor and in rags,
Rather than wealthy and not free.

The rain and wind are hard masters;
I have known you wince under their lash.
But there was comfort for you at the day's end
Dreaming over the warm ash

Of a turf fire on a hill farm,
Contented with your accustomed ration
Of bread and bacon, and drawing your strength
From membership of an old nation

Not given to beg. But look at yourself
Now, a servant hired to flog
The life out of the slow soil,
Or come obediently as a dog

To the pound's whistle. Can't you see
Behind the smile on the times' face
The cold brain of the machine
That will destroy you and your race?

Hireling

Cars pass him by; he'll never own one.
Men won't believe in him for this.
Let them come into the hills
And meet him wandering a road,
Fenced with rain, as I have now;
The wind feathering his hair;
The sky's ruins, gutted with fire
Of the late sun, smouldering still.

Nothing is his, neither the land
Nor the land's flocks. Hired to live
On hills too lonely, sharing his hearth
With cats and hens, he has lost all
Property but the grey ice
Of a face splintered by life's stone.

Lore

Job Davies, eighty-five
Winters old, and still alive
After the slow poison
And treachery of the seasons.

Miserable? Kick my arse!
It needs more than the rain's hearse,
Wind-drawn, to pull me off
The great perch of my laugh.

What's living but courage?
Paunch full of hot porridge,
Nerves strengthened with tea,
Peat-black, dawn found me

Mowing where the grass grew,
Bearded with golden dew.
Rhythm of the long scythe
Kept this tall frame lithe.

What to do? Stay green.
Never mind the machine,
Whose fuel is human souls.
Live large, man, and dream small.

A Welsh Testament

All right, I was Welsh. Does it matter?
I spoke the tongue that was passed on
To me in the place I happened to be,
A place huddled between grey walls
Of cloud for at least half the year.
My word for heaven was not yours.
The word for hell had a sharp edge
Put on it by the hand of the wind
Honing, honing with a shrill sound
Day and night. Nothing that Glyn Dŵr
Knew was armour against the rain's
Missiles. What was descent from him?

Even God had a Welsh name:
We spoke to him in the old language;
He was to have a peculiar care
For the Welsh people. History showed us
He was too big to be nailed to the wall
Of a stone chapel, yet still we crammed him
Between the boards of a black book.

Yet men sought us despite this.
My high cheek-bones, my length of skull
Drew them as to a rare portrait
By a dead master. I saw them stare
From their long cars, as I passed knee-deep
In ewes and wethers. I saw them stand
By the thorn hedges, watching me string
The far flocks on a shrill whistle.
And always there was their eyes' strong
Pressure on me: You are Welsh, they said;
Speak to us so; keep your fields free
Of the smell of petrol, the loud roar
Of hot tractors; we must have peace
And quietness.
                    Is a museum

Peace? I asked. Am I the keeper
Of the heart's relics, blowing the dust
In my own eyes? I am a man;
I never wanted the drab rôle
Life assigned me, an actor playing
To the past's audience upon a stage
Of earth and stone; the absurd label
Of birth, of race hanging askew
About my shoulders. I was in prison
Until you came; your voice was a key
Turning in the enormous lock
Of hopelessness. Did the door open
To let me out or yourselves in?

Here

I am a man now.
Pass your hand over my brow,
You can feel the place where the brains grow.

I am like a tree,
From my top boughs I can see
The footprints that led up to me.

There is blood in my veins
That has run clear of the stain
Contracted in so many loins.

Why, then, are my hands red
With the blood of so many dead?
Is this where I was misled?

Why are my hands this way
That they will not do as I say?
Does no God hear when I pray?

I have nowhere to go.
The swift satellites show
The clock of my whole being is slow.

It is too late to start
For destinations not of the heart.
I must stay here with my hurt.

To a Young Poet

For the first twenty years you are still growing,
Bodily that is; as a poet, of course,
You are not born yet. It's the next ten
You cut your teeth on to emerge smirking
For your brash courtship of the muse.
You will take seriously those first affairs
With young poems, but no attachments
Formed then but come to shame you,
When love has changed to a grave service
Of a cold queen.
                        From forty on
You learn from the sharp cuts and jags
Of poems that have come to pieces
In your crude hands how to assemble
With more skill the arbitrary parts
Of ode or sonnet, while time fosters
A new impulse to conceal your wounds
From her and from a bold public,
Given to pry.
                        You are old now
As years reckon, but in that slower
World of the poet you are just coming
To sad manhood, knowing the smile
On her proud face is not for you.

Tramp

A knock at the door
And he stands there,
A tramp with his can
Asking for tea,
Strong for a poor man
On his way – where?

He looks at his feet,
I look at the sky;
Over us the planes build
The shifting rafters
Of that new world
We have sworn by.

I sleep in my bed,
He sleeps in the old,
Dead leaves of a ditch.
My dreams are haunted;
Are his dreams rich?
If I wake early,
He wakes cold.

Servant

You served me well, Prytherch.
From all my questionings and doubts;
From brief acceptance of the times'
Deities; from ache of the mind
Or body's tyranny, I turned,
Often after a whole year,
Often twice in the same day,
To where you read in the slow book
Of the farm, turning the fields' pages
So patiently, never tired
Of the land's story; not just believing,
But proving in your bone and your blood
Its accuracy; willing to stand
Always aside from the main road,
Where life's flashier illustrations
Were marginal.
                        Not that you gave
The whole answer. Is truth so bare,
So dark, so dumb, as on your hearth
And in your company I found it?
Is not the evolving print of the sky
To be read, too; the mineral
Of the mind worked? Is not truth choice,
With a clear eye and a free hand,
From life's bounty?
                           Not choice for you,
But seed sown upon the thin
Soil of a heart, not rich, nor fertile,
Yet capable of the one crop,
Which is the bread of truth that I break.

On the Farm

There was Dai Puw. He was no good.
They put him in the fields to dock swedes,
And took the knife from him, when he came home
At late evening with a grin
Like the slash of a knife on his face.

There was Llew Puw, and he was no good.
Every evening after the ploughing
With the big tractor he would sit in his chair,
And stare into the tangled fire garden,
Opening his slow lips like a snail.

There was Huw Puw, too. What shall I say?
I have heard him whistling in the hedges
On and on, as though winter
Would never again leave those fields,
And all the trees were deformed.

And lastly there was the girl:
Beauty under some spell of the beast.
Her pale face was the lantern
By which they read in life's dark book
The shrill sentence: God is love.

Amen

And God said: How do you know?
And I went out into the fields
At morning and it was true.

Nothing denied it, neither the bowed man
On his knees, nor the animals,
Nor the birds notched on the sky's

Surface. His heart was broken
Far back, and the beasts yawned
Their boredom. Under the song

Of the larks, I heard the wheels turn
Rustily. But the scene held;
The cold landscape returned my stare;

There was no answer. Accept; accept.
And under the green capitals,
The molecules and the blood's virus.

Gifts

From my father my strong heart,
My weak stomach.
From my mother the fear.

From my sad country the shame.

To my wife all I have
Saving only the love
That is not mine to give.

To my one son the hunger.

A Welshman
at St James' Park

I am invited to enter these gardens
As one of the public, and to conduct myself
In accordance with the regulations;
To keep off the grass and sample flowers
Without touching them; to admire birds
That have been seduced from wildness by
Bread they are pelted with.
                       I am not one
Of the public; I have come a long way
To realise it. Under the sun's
Feathers are the sinews of stone,
The curved claws.
                    I think of a Welsh hill
That is without fencing, and the men,
Bosworth blind, who left the heather
And the high pastures of the heart. I fumble
In the pocket's emptiness; my ticket
Was in two pieces. I kept half.

Service

We stand looking at
Each other. I take the word 'prayer'
And present it to them. I wait idly,
Wondering what their lips will
Make of it. But they hand back
Such presents. I am left alone
With no echoes to the amen
I dreamed of. I am saved by music
From the emptiness of this place
Of despair. As the melody rises
From nothing, their mouths take up the tune,
And the roof listens. I call on God
In the after silence, and my shadow
Wrestles with him upon a wall
Of plaster, that has all the nation's
Hardness in it. They see me thrown
Without movement of their oblique eyes.

In Church

Often I try
To analyse the quality
Of its silences. Is this where God hides
From my searching? I have stopped to listen,
After the few people have gone,
To the air recomposing itself
For vigil. It has waited like this
Since the stones grouped themselves about it.
These are the hard ribs
Of a body that our prayers have failed
To animate. Shadows advance
From their corners to take possession
Of places the light held
For an hour. The bats resume
Their business. The uneasiness of the pews
Ceases. There is no other sound
In the darkness but the sound of a man
Breathing, testing his faith
On emptiness, nailing his questions
One by one to an untenanted cross.

Reservoirs

There are places in Wales I don't go:
Reservoirs that are the subconscious
Of a people, troubled far down
With gravestones, chapels, villages even;
The serenity of their expression
Revolts me, it is a pose
For strangers, a watercolour's appeal
To the mass, instead of the poem's
Harsher conditions. There are the hills,
Too; gardens gone under the scum
Of the forests; and the smashed faces
Of the farms with the stone trickle
Of their tears down the hills' side.

Where can I go, then, from the smell
Of decay, from the putrefying of a dead
Nation? I have walked the shore
For an hour and seen the English
Scavenging among the remains
Of our culture, covering the sand
Like the tide and, with the roughness
Of the tide, elbowing our language
Into the grave that we have dug for it.

Welcome to Wales

Come to Wales
To be buried; the undertaker
Will arrange it for you. We have
The sites and a long line
Of clients going back
To the first milkman who watered
His honour. How they endow
Our country with their polished
Memorials! No one lives
In our villages, but they dream
Of returning from the rigours
Of the pound's climate. Why not
Try it? We can always raise
Some mourners, and the amens
Are ready. This is what
Chapels are for; their varnish
Wears well and will go
With most coffins. Let us
Quote you; our terms
Are the lowest, and we offer,
Dirt cheap, a place where
It is lovely to lie.

Kneeling

Moments of great calm,
Kneeling before an altar
Of wood in a stone church
In summer, waiting for the God
To speak; the air a staircase
For silence; the sun's light
Ringing me, as though I acted
A great rôle. And the audiences
Still; all that close throng
Of spirits waiting, as I,
For the message.
                        Prompt me, God;
But not yet. When I speak,
Though it be you who speak
Through me, something is lost.
The meaning is in the waiting.

They

I take their hands,
Hard hands. There is no love
For such, only a willed
Gentleness. Negligible men
From the village, from the small
Holdings, they bring their grief
Sullenly to my back door,
And are speechless. Seeing them
In the wind with the light's
Halo, watching their eyes
Blur, I know the reason
They cry, their worsting
By one whom they will fight.

Daily the sky mirrors
The water, the water the
Sky. Daily I take their side
In their quarrel, calling their faults
Mine. How do I serve so
This being they have shut out
Of their houses, their thoughts, their lives?

Once

God looked at space and I appeared,
Rubbing my eyes at what I saw.
The earth smoked, no birds sang;
There were no footprints on the beaches
Of the hot sea, no creatures in it.
God spoke. I hid myself in the side
Of the mountain.

                    As though born again
I stepped out into the cool dew,
Trying to remember the fire sermon,
Astonished at the mingled chorus
Of weeds and flowers. In the brown bark
Of the trees I saw the many faces
Of life, forms hungry for birth,
Mouthing at me. I held my way
To the light, inspecting my shadow
Boldly; and in the late morning
You, rising towards me out of the depths
Of myself. I took your hand,
Remembering you, and together,
Confederates of the natural day,
We went forth to meet the Machine.

Echoes

What is this? said God. The obstinacy
Of its refusal to answer
Enraged him. He struck it
Those great blows it resounds
With still. It glowered at
Him, but remained dumb,
Turning on its slow axis
Of pain, reflecting the year
In its seasons. Nature bandaged
Its wounds. Healing in
The smooth sun, it became
Fair. God looked at it
Again, reminded of
An intention. They shall answer
For you, he said. And at once
There were trees with birds
Singing, and through the trees
Animals wandered, drinking
Their own scent, conceding
An absence. Where are you?
He called, and riding the echo
The shapes came, slender
As trees, but with white hands,
Curious to build. On the altars
They made him the red blood
Told what he wished to hear.

Digest

Mostly it was wars
With their justification
Of the surrender of values
For which they fought. Between
Them they laid their plans
For the next, exempted
From compact by the machine's
Exigencies. Silence
Was out of date; wisdom consisted
In a revision of the strict code
Of the spirit. To keep moving
Was best; to bring the arrival
Nearer departure; to synchronise
The applause, as the public images
Stepped on and off the stationary
Aircraft. The labour of the years
Was over; the children were heirs
To an instant existence. They fed the machine
Their questions, knowing the answers
Already, unable to apply them.

The Island

And God said, I will build a church here
And cause this people to worship me,
And afflict them with poverty and sickness
In return for centuries of hard work
And patience. And its walls shall be hard as
Their hearts, and its windows let in the light
Grudgingly, as their minds do, and the priest's words be drowned
By the wind's caterwauling. All this I will do,

Said God, and watch the bitterness in their eyes
Grow, and their lips suppurate with
Their prayers. And their women shall bring forth
On my altars, and I will choose the best
Of them to be thrown back into the sea.

And that was only on one island.

The Coming

And God held in his hand
A small globe. Look, he said.
The son looked. Far off,
As through water, he saw
A scorched land of fierce
Colour. The light burned
There; crusted buildings
Cast their shadows; a bright
Serpent, a river
Uncoiled itself, radiant
With slime.
         On a bare
Hill a bare tree saddened
The sky. Many people
Held out their thin arms
To it, as though waiting
For a vanished April
To return to its crossed
Boughs. The son watched
Them. Let me go there, he said.

Madam

And if you ask her
She has no name;
But her eyes say,
Water is cold.

She is three years old
And willing to kiss;
But her lips say,
Apples are sour.

Circles

A man threw some brushings away.
A wren found them and built in them.
A rat found the young when they were hatched.
The rat came, stealing the man's bread,
And lies now, a cupboard for maggots.

It is man makes the first move and the last.
He throws things away and they return to him.
He seeks things that always withdraw
And finds them waiting on his return.
He takes his departure from God
And is as trash thrown away.
But a dream finds him and builds in him,
And death comes and eats up the dreamer's
Brood. And still it is out of a man
Death is born; so before death
Man is, and after death
There is more man, and the dream outlasts
Death, and the dreamer will never die.

To Pay for His Keep

So this was on the way
to a throne! He looked round
at the perspiring ranks
of ageing respectacles:
police, tradesmen, councillors,
rigid with imagined
loyalty; and beyond them at
the town with its mean streets and
pavements filthy with
dog shit.
        The castle was
huge. All that dead weight
of the past, that overloading
of the law's mounting
equipment! A few medals
would do now. He permitted
himself a small smile,
sipping at it in the mind's
coolness.
        And never noticed,
because of the dust raised
by the prayers of the fagged
clergy, that far hill
in the sun with the long line
of its trees climbing
it like a procession
of young people, young as himself.

His Condescensions Are Short-Lived

I don't know, he said. I feel sorry
for the English – a fine people
in some ways, but victims
of their traditions. All those tanks
and guns; the processions
that go nowhere; the medals
and gold braid; the government's
yearly awards; the replenishment
of the clapped ranks of
the peerage. Democracy is the tip
the rich and the well-born give
for your homage.
                         I admired him
there, as he sat nonchalantly
in his chair, flicking the ash from
his cigarette – supplied, by the way,
as most things in Wales are
supplied, by English wholesalers.

Emerging

Not as in the old days I pray,
God. My life is not what it was.
Yours, too, accepts the presence of
the machine? Once I would have asked
healing. I go now to be doctored,
to drink sinlessly of the blood
of my brother, to lend my flesh
as manuscript of the great poem
of the scalpel. I would have knelt
long, wrestling with you, wearing
you down. Hear my prayer, Lord, hear
my prayer. As though you were deaf, myriads
of mortals have kept up their shrill
cry, explaining your silence by
their unfitness.

               It begins to appear
this is not what prayer is about.
It is the annihilation of difference,
the consciousness of myself in you,
of you in me; the emerging
from the adolescence of nature
into the adult geometry
of the mind. I begin to recognise
you anew, God of form and number.
There are questions we are the solution
to, others whose echoes we must expand
to contain. Circular as our way
is, it leads not back to that snake-haunted
garden, but onward to the tall city
of glass that is the laboratory of the spirit.

Amen

It was all arranged:
the virgin with child, the birth
in Bethlehem, the arid journey uphill
to Jerusalem. The prophets foretold
it, the scriptures conditioned him
to accept it. Judas went to his work
with his sour kiss; what else
could he do?
                    A wise old age,
the honours awarded for lasting,
are not for a saviour. He had
to be killed; salvation acquired
by an increased guilt. The tree,
with its roots in the mind's dark,
was divinely planted, the original fork
in existence. There is no meaning in life
unless men can be found to reject
love. God needs his martyrdom.
The mild eyes stare from the Cross
in perverse triumph. What does he care
that the people's offerings are so small?

Poste Restante

I want you to know how it was,
whether the Cross grinds into dust
under men's wheels or shines brightly
as a monument to a new era.

There was a church and one man
served it, and few worshipped
there in the raw light on the hill
in winter, moving among the stones
fallen about them like the ruins
of a culture they were too weak
to replace, too poor themselves
to do anything but wait
for the ending of a life
they had not asked for.
                         The priest would come
and pull on the hoarse bell nobody
heard, and enter that place
of darkness, sour with the mould
of the years. And the spider would run
from the chalice, and the wine lie
there for a time, cold and unwanted
by all but he, while the candles
guttered as the wind picked
at the roof. And he would see
over that bare meal his face
staring at him from the cracked glass
of the window, with the lips moving
like those of an inhabitant of
a world beyond this.
                     And so back
to the damp vestry to the book
where he would scratch his name and the date
he could hardly remember, Sunday
by Sunday, while the place sank
to its knees and the earth turned

from season to season like the wheel
of a great foundry to produce
you, friend, who will know what happened.

The Chapel

A little aside from the main road,
becalmed in a last-century greyness,
there is the chapel, ugly, without the appeal
to the tourist to stop his car
and visit it. The traffic goes by,
and the river goes by, and quick shadows
of clouds, too, and the chapel settles
a little deeper into the grass.

But here once on an evening like this,
in the darkness that was about
his hearers, a preacher caught fire
and burned steadily before them
with a strange light, so that they saw
the splendour of the barren mountains
about them and sang their amens
fiercely, narrow but saved
in a way that men are not now.

The Moon in Lleyn

The last quarter of the moon
of Jesus gives way
to the dark; the serpent
digests the egg. Here
on my knees in this stone
church, that is full only
of the silent congregation
of shadows and the sea's
sound, it is easy to believe
Yeats was right. Just as though
choirs had not sung, shells
have swallowed them; the tide laps
at the Bible; the bell fetches
no people to the brittle miracle
of the bread. The sand is waiting
for the running back of the grains
in the wall into its blond
glass. Religion is over, and
what will emerge from the body
of the new moon, no one
can say.
          But a voice sounds
in my ear: Why so fast,
mortal? These very seas
are baptised. The parish
has a saint's name time cannot
unfrock. In cities that
have outgrown their promise people
are becoming pilgrims
again, if not to this place,
then to the recreation of it
in their own spirits. You must remain
kneeling. Even as this moon
making its way through the earth's
cumbersome shadow, prayer, too,
has its phases.

The Gap

The one thing they were not troubled
by was perfection; it was theirs
already. Their hand moved in the dark
like a priest's, giving its blessing
to the bare wall. Drawings appeared
there like a violation of the privacy
of the creatures. They withdrew with their work
finished, leaving the interrogation of it
to ourselves, who inherit everything
but their genius.
                    This was before
the fall. Somewhere between them and us
the mind climbed up into the tree
of knowledge, and saw the forbidden subjects
of art, the emptiness of the interiors
of the mirror that life holds up
to itself, and began venting its frustration
in spurious metals, in the cold acts of the machine.

Which

And in the book I read:
God is love. But lifting
my head, I do not find it
so. Shall I return

to my book and, between
print, wander an air
heavy with the scent
of this one word? Or not trust

language, only the blows that
life gives me, wearing them
like those red tokens with which
an agreement is sealed?

Gone

There was a flower blowing
and a hand plucked it.

There was a stream flowing
and a body smirched it.

There was a pure mirror
of water and a face came

and looked in it. There were words
and wars and treaties, and feet trampled

the earth and the wheels
seared it; and an explosion

followed. There was dust
and silence; and out of the dust

a plant grew, and the dew formed
upon it; and a stream seeped

from the dew to construct
a mirror, and the mirror was empty.

Pardon

What pardon for this, Lord?

There was a man ate bread
from your hand and did not snap
at it; but when on his knees
listened to the snivelling sound
of laughter from somewhere inside
himself. He had been taught
that to laugh was an echo
of the divine joy; but this
was the lifting of a dog's leg
in a temple. There is no defence
against laughter issuing
at the wrong time, but is there ever
forgiveness?
        He went from his prayers
into a world holding
its sides, but the return
to them was the return
to vomit, thanking where
he did not believe for something
he did not want but could not
refuse.
    There is no pardon
for this, only the expedient
of blaming the laughter on someone else.

The Bright Field

I have seen the sun break through
to illuminate a small field
for a while, and gone my way
and forgotten it. But that was the pearl
of great price, the one field that had
the treasure in it. I realize now
that I must give all that I have
to possess it. Life is not hurrying

on to a receding future, nor hankering after
an imagined past. It is the turning
aside like Moses to the miracle
of the lit bush, to a brightness
that seemed as transitory as your youth
once, but is the eternity that awaits you.

Good

The old man comes out on the hill
and looks down to recall earlier days
in the valley. He sees the stream shine,
the church stand, hears the litter of
children's voices. A chill in the flesh
tells him that death is not far off
now: it is the shadow under the great boughs
of life. His garden has herbs growing.
The kestrel goes by with fresh prey
in its claws. The wind scatters the scent
of wild beans. The tractor operates
on the earth's body. His grandson is there
ploughing; his young wife fetches him
cakes and tea and a dark smile. It is well.

The Way of It

With her fingers she turns paint
into flowers, with her body
flowers into a remembrance
of herself. She is at work
always, mending the garment
of our marriage, foraging
like a bird for something
for us to eat. If there are thorns
in my life, it is she who
will press her breast to them and sing.

Her words, when she would scold,
are too sharp. She is busy
after for hours rubbing smiles
into the wounds. I saw her,
when young, and spread the panoply
of my feathers instinctively
to engage her. She was not deceived,
but accepted me as a girl
will under a thin moon
in love's absence as someone
she could build a home with
for her imagined child.

The Gap

God woke, but the nightmare
did not recede. Word by word
the tower of speech grew.
He looked at it from the air
he reclined on. One word more and
it would be on a level
with him; vocabulary
would have triumphed. He
measured the thin gap
with his mind. No, no, no,
wider than that! But the nearness
persisted. How to live with
the fact, that was the feat
now. How to take his rest
on the edge of a chasm a
word could bridge.
                  He leaned
over and looked in the dictionary
they used. There was the blank still
by his name of the same
order as the territory
between them, the verbal hunger
for the thing in itself. And the darkness
that is a god's blood swelled
in him, and he let it
to make the sign in the space
on the page, that is in all languages
and none; that is the grammarian's
torment and the mystery
at the cell's core, and the equation
that will not come out, and is
the narrowness that we stare
over into the eternal
silence that is the repose of God.

Fishing

Sometimes I go out with the small men
with dark faces and let my line
down quietly into the water, meditating
as they do for hours on end

on the nature and destiny of fish,
of how they are many and other and good
to eat, willing them by a sort of personal
magic to attach themselves to my hook.

The water is deep. Sometimes from far
down invisible messages arrive.
Often it seems it is for more than fish
that we seek; we wait for the

withheld answer to an insoluble
problem. Life is short. The sea starts
where the land ends; its surface
is all flowers, but within are the

grim inmates. The line trembles; mostly,
when we would reel in the catch, there
is nothing to see. The hook gleams, the
smooth face creases in an obscene

grin. But we fish on, and gradually
they accumulate, the bodies, in the torn
light that is about us and the air
echoes to their inaudible screaming.

Groping

Moving away is only to the boundaries
of the self. Better to stay here,
I said, leaving the horizons
clear. The best journey to make
is inward. It is the interior
that calls. Eliot heard it.
Wordsworth turned from the great hills
of the north to the precipice
of his own mind, and let himself
down for the poetry stranded
on the bare ledges.
                              For some
it is all darkness; for me, too,
it is dark. But there are hands
there I can take, voices to hear
solider than the echoes
without. And sometimes a strange light
shines, purer than the moon,
casting no shadow, that is
the halo upon the bones
of the pioneers who died for truth.

At It

I think he sits at that strange table
of Eddington's, that is not a table
at all, but nodes and molecules
pushing against molecules
and nodes; and he writes there
in invisible handwriting the instructions
the genes follow. I imagine his
face that is more the face
of a clock, and the time told by it
is now, though Greece is referred
to and Egypt and empires
not yet begun.
           And I would have
things to say to this God
at the judgement, storming at him,
as Job stormed, with the eloquence
of the abused heart. But there will be
no judgement other than the verdict
of his calculations, that abstruse
geometry that proceeds eternally
in the silence beyond right and wrong.

The Truce

That they should not advance
beyond certain limits left –
accidentally? – undefined;
and that compensation be paid
by the other side. Meanwhile the
peasant – There are no peasants
in Wales, he said, holding
his liquor as a gentleman
should not – went up and down
his acre, rejecting the pot
of gold at the rainbow's
end in favour of earthier
values: the subsidies gradually
propagating themselves on the guilt
of an urban class.
                              Strenuous
times! Never all day
did the procession of popular
images through the farm
kitchens cease; it was tiring
watching. Such truce as was
called in the invisible
warfare between bad and
worse was where two half-truths
faced one another over
the body of an exhausted
nation, each one waiting for
the other to be proved wrong.

Dialectic

They spoke to him in Hebrew and he understood
them; in Latin and Italian and
he understood them. Speech palled
on them and they turned to the silence
of their equations. But God listened to them
as to a spider spinning its web
from its entrails, the mind swinging
to and fro over an abysm
of blankness. They are speaking to me still,
he decided, in the geometry
I delight in, in the figures
that beget more figures. I will answer
them as of old with the infinity
I feed on. If there were words once
they could not understand, I will show
them now space that is bounded
but without end, time that is where
they were or will be; the eternity
that is here for me and for them
there; the truth that with much labour
is born with them and is to be
sloughed off like some afterbirth of the spirit.

The Signpost

Casgob, it said, 2
miles. But I never went
there; left it like an ornament
on the mind's shelf, covered

with the dust of
its summers; a place on a diet
of the echoes of stopped
bells and children's

voices; white the architecture
of its clouds, stationary
its sunlight. It was best
so. I need a museum

for storing the dream's
brittler particles in. Time
is a main road, eternity
the turning that we don't take.

Gone?

Will they say on some future
occasion, looking over the flogged acres
of ploughland: This was Prytherch country?
Nothing to show for it now: hedges
uprooted, walls gone, a mobile people
hurrying to and fro on their fast
tractors; a forest of aerials
as though an invading fleet invisibly
had come to anchor among these
financed hills. They copy the image
of themselves projected on their smooth
screens to the accompaniment of inane
music. They give grins and smiles
back in return for the money that is
spent on them. But where is the face
with the crazed eyes that through the unseen
drizzle of its tears looked out
on this land and found no beauty
in it, but accepted it, as a man
will who has needs in him that only
bare ground, black thorns and the sky's
                                    emptiness can fulfil?

The Empty Church

They laid this stone trap
for him, enticing him with candles,
as though he would come like some huge moth
out of the darkness to beat there.
Ah, he had burned himself
before in the human flame
and escaped, leaving the reason
torn. He will not come any more

to our lure. Why, then, do I kneel still
striking my prayers on a stone
heart? Is it in hope one
of them will ignite yet and throw
on its illumined walls the shadow
of someone greater than I can understand?

The Absence

It is this great absence
that is like a presence, that compels
me to address it without hope
of a reply. It is a room I enter

from which someone has just
gone, the vestibule for the arrival
of one who has not yet come.
I modernise the anachronism

of my language, but he is no more here
than before. Genes and molecules
have no more power to call
him up than the incense of the Hebrews

at their altars. My equations fail
as my words do. What resource have I
other than the emptiness without him of my whole
being, a vacuum he may not abhor?

Covenant

I feel sometimes
          we are his penance
for having made us. He
suffers in us and we partake
          of his suffering. What
to do, when it has been done
          already? Where
          to go, when the arrival
is as the departure? Circularity
is a mental condition, the
animals know nothing of it.

          Seven times have passed
over him, and he is still here.
          When will he return
from his human exile, and will
peace then be restored
          to the flesh?
                              Often
I think that there is no end
to this torment and that the electricity
that convulses us is the fire
          in which a god
burns and is not consumed.

Adder

What is this creature discarded
like a toy necklace
among the weeds and flowers,
singing to me silently

of the fire never to be put out
at its thin lips? It is scion
of a mighty ancestor
that spoke the language

of trees to our first
parents and greened its scales
in the forbidden one, timelessly shining
as though autumn were never to be.

Centuries

The fifteenth passes with drums and in armour;
the monk watches it through the mind's grating.

The sixteenth puts on its cap and bells
to poach vocabulary from a king's laughter.

The seventeenth wears a collar of lace
at its neck, the flesh running from thought's candle.

The eighteenth has a high fever and hot blood,
but clears its nostrils with the snuff of wit.

The nineteenth emerges from history's cave
rubbing its eyes at the glass prospect.

The twentieth is what it looked forward to
beating its wings at windows that are not there.

Suddenly

Suddenly after long silence
he has become voluble.
He addresses me from a myriad
directions with the fluency
of water, the articulateness
of green leaves; and in the genes,
too, the components
of my existence. The rock,
so long speechless, is the library
of his poetry. He sings to me
in the chain-saw, writes
with the surgeon's hand
on the skin's parchment messages
of healing. The weather
is his mind's turbine
driving the earth's bulk round
and around on its remedial
journey. I have no need
to despair; as at
some second Pentecost
of a Gentile, I listen to the things
round me: weeds, stones, instruments,
the machine itself, all
speaking to me in the vernacular
of the purposes of One who is.

Arrival

Not conscious
        that you have been seeking
                suddenly
        you come upon it

the village in the Welsh hills
                dust free
        with no road out
but the one you came in by.

        A bird chimes
    from a green tree
the hour that is no hour
        you know. The river dawdles
to hold a mirror for you
where you may see yourself
        as you are, a traveller
                with the moon's halo
        above him, who has arrived
        after long journeying where he
                began, catching this
        one truth by surprise
that there is everything to look forward to.

Brother

It came into being.
From eternity? In
time? Was the womb
prepared for it, or it
for the womb? It lay in the cradle
long months, staring its world
into a shape, decorated
with faces. It addressed
objects, preferred its vocabulary
to their own; grew eloquent
before a resigned
audience. It was fed
speech and vomited
it and was not reproved.
It began walking,
falling, bruising itself
on the bone's truth. The fire
was a tart playmate. It
was taken in by the pool's smile.
Need I go on? It survived
its disasters; met fact
with the mind's guile; forged
for itself wings, missiles.
Launched itself on a dark
night through the nursery
window into adult orbit
out of the reach of gravity's control.

Sonata

Evening. The wind rising.
The gathering excitement
of the leaves, and Beethoven
on the piano, chords reverberating
in our twin being.
                    'What is life?'
pitifully her eyes
asked. And I who was no seer
took hold of her loth hand
and examined it and was lost
like a pure mathematician
in its solution: strokes
cancelling strokes: angles
bisected; the line of life deviating
from the line of the head; a way
that was laid down for her to walk
which was not my way.
                    While the music
went on and on with chromatic
insistence, passionately proclaiming
by the keys' moonlight in the darkening
drawing-room how our art is our meaning.

The Unvanquished

And courage shall give way
to despair and despair
to suffering, and suffering
shall end in death. But you
who are not free to choose
what you suffer can choose
your response. Farmers I
knew, born to the ills
of their kind, scrubbed bare
by the weather, suffocating
with phlegm; all their means gone
to buy their consumptive son
the profession his body
could not sustain. Proudly
they lived, watching the spirit,
diamond-faceted, crumble
to the small, hard, round, dry
stone that humanity
chokes on. When they died, it
was bravely, close up under the rain-hammered
rafters, never complaining.

Destinations

Travelling towards the light
we were waylaid by darkness;
a formless company detained us,
saying everything, meaning nothing.

It is a conspiracy, I said,
of great age, in revolt
against reason, against all
that would be ethereal in us.

We looked at one another.
Was it the silence of agreement,
or the vacuum between two minds
not in contact? There is an ingredient

in thought that is its own
hindrance. Had we come all that way
to detect it? The voices combined,
urging us to put our trust

in the bone's wisdom. Remember,
they charged us, the future
for which you are bound is where
you began. Was there a counter

command? I listened as to
a tideless sea on a remote
star, and knew our direction
was elsewhere; to the light, yes,

but not such as minerals
deploy; to the brightness over
an interior horizon, which is science
transfiguring itself in love's mirror.

The Other

There are nights that are so still
that I can hear the small owl calling
far off and a fox barking
miles away. It is then that I lie
in the lean hours awake listening
to the swell born somewhere in the Atlantic
rising and falling, rising and falling
wave on wave on the long shore
by the village, that is without light
and companionless. And the thought comes
of that other being who is awake, too,
letting our prayers break on him,
not like this for a few hours,
but for days, years, for eternity.

Drowning

They were irreplaceable and forgettable,
inhabitants of the parish and speakers
of the Welsh tongue. I looked on and
there was one less and one less and one less.

They were not of the soil, but contributed
to it in dying, a manure not
to be referred to as such, but from which
poetry is grown and legends and green tales.

Their immortality was what they hoped for
by being kind. Their smiles were such as,
exercised so often, became perennial
as flowers, blossoming where they had been cut down.

I ministered uneasily among them until
what had been gaps in the straggling hedgerow
of the nation widened to reveal the emptiness
that was inside, where echoes haunted and thin ghosts.

A rare place, but one identifiable
with other places where on as deep a sea
men have clung to the last spars of their language
and gone down with it, unremembered but uncomplaining.

Testimonies

The first stood up and testified to Christ:
I was made in the image of man; he unmanned me.

The second stood up: He appeared to me
in church in a stained window. I saw through him.

The third: Patient of love, I went
to him with my infirmity, and was not cured.

The fourth stood up, with between his thighs
a sword. 'He came not to bring peace' he said.

The fifth, child of his time, wasted his time
asking eternity: 'Who is my father and mother?'

So all twelve spoke, parodies of the disciples
on their way to those bone thrones from which they
      would judge others.

Looking Glass

There is a game I play
with a mirror, approaching
it when I am not there,
as though to take by surprise

the self that is my familiar. It
is in vain. Like one eternally
in ambush, fast or slow
as I may raise my head, it raises

its own, catching me in the act,
disarming me by acquaintance,
looking full into my face as often
as I try looking at it askance.

Unposted

Dear friend unknown,
why send me your poems?
We are brothers, I admit;
but they are no good.
I see why you wrote them,
but why send them? Why not
bury them, as a cat its faeces?
You confuse charity and art.
They have not equal claims,
though the absence of either
will smell more or less the same.

I use my imagination:
I see a cramped hand gripping
a bent pen, or, worse perhaps,
it was with your foot you wrote.
You wait in an iron bed
for my reply. My letter
could be the purse of gold
you pay your way with past
the giant, Despair.
                       I lower my standards
and let truth hit me squarely
between the eyes. 'These are great
poems,' I write, and see heaven's
slums with their rags flying,
cripples brandishing their crutches,
and the one, innocent of scansion,
who knows charity is short
and the poem for ever, suffering
my dark lie with all the blandness
with which the round moon suffers an eclipse.

This One

Sometimes a shadow passed
between him and the light.
Sometimes a light showed itself
in the darkness beyond. Could
it be? The strong angels wrestled
and were not disposed to give
him the verdict. Are there journeys
without destinations? The animals
paused and became gargoyles
beside the way. And this one,
standing apart to confer
with the eternal, was he blamed
for reaction? There is always
laughter out of the speeding
vehicles for the man
who is still, half-way though he be
in a better direction. From receding
horizons he has withdrawn
his mind for greater repose
on an inner perspective,
where love is the bridge between
thought and time. Consumers
of distance at vast cost,
what do they know of the green
twig with which he divines,
where life balances excess
of death, the bottomless
water that is the soul's glass?

Truly

No, I was not born
to refute Hume, to write
the first poem with no
noun. My gift was

for evasion, taking
cover at the approach
of greatness, as of
ill-fame. I looked truth

in the eye, and was not
abashed at discovering
it squinted. I fasted
at import's table, so had

an appetite for the banal,
the twelve baskets full left
over after the turning
of the little into so much.

A Marriage

We met
        under a shower
of bird-notes.
        Fifty years passed,
love's moment
        in a world in
servitude to time.
        She was young;
I kissed with my eyes
        closed and opened
them on her wrinkles.
        'Come,' said death,
choosing her as his
        partner for
the last dance. And she,
        who in life
had done everything
        with a bird's grace,
opened her bill now
        for the shedding
of one sigh no
        heavier than a feather.